# DISNEY
# FROZEN II

Set three years after the events of *Frozen*, *Frozen 2* begins when Elsa hears a strange calling from the north. Joining her sister Anna, and her friends Kristoff, Olaf, and Sven, Elsa embarks on an epic adventure beyond Arendelle and into the unknown...

In this deluxe collectors' volume, we look at how the talented team behind the movie created the highly-anticipated sequel to the biggest animated hit of all-time.

**COLLECT THE OFFICIAL DISNEY SPECIALS**

*Dumbo*
*Toy Story 4*
*The Lion King*

FROZEN 2 The Official Movie Special
ISBN: 9781787731844
First published November 2019

**DISTRIBUTION**
US Newsstand: Total Publisher Services, Inc.
John Dziewiatkowski, 630-851-7683
US Newsstand Distribution: Curtis Circulation Company
US Bookstore Distribution: The News Group
US Direct Sales Market: Diamond Comic Distributors

For info on advertising contact adinfo@titanemail.com

**PRINTED IN THE US BY QUAD.**

TITAN EDITORIAL: Jonathan Wilkins, Martin Eden, Donna Askem, Phoebe Hedges, Darryl Tothill, Leigh Baulch, Vivian Cheung, Nick Landau.

CONTRIBUTORS: Abbie Bernstein, Dan Jolin, Nick Jones.

THANK YOU to Christopher Troise, Shiho Tilley, Eugene Paraszczuk and all at Disney.

DISNEY PUBLISHING WORLDWIDE
Global Magazines, Comics and Partworks Publisher: Lynn Waggoner. Editorial Team: Bianca Coletti (Director, Magazines), Guido Frazzini (Director, Comics), Stefano Ambrosio (Executive Editor, New IP), Carlotta Quattrocolo (Executive Editor), Camilla Vedove (Senior Manager, Editorial Development), Behnoosh Khalili (Senior Editor), Julie Dorris (Senior Editor), Mina Riazi (Assistant Editor). Gabriela Capasso (assistant editor), Design: Enrico Soave (Senior Designer). Art: Ken Shue (VP, Global Art), Roberto Santillo (Creative Director), Marco Ghiglione (Creative Manager), Manny Mederos (Senior Illustration Manager), Stefano Attardi (Illustration Manager). Portfolio Management: Olivia Ciancarelli (Director). Business

& Marketing: Mariantonietta Galla (Senior Manager, Franchise), Virpi Korhonen (Editorial Manager).

A CIP catalogue record for this title is available from the British Library.

TITAN
MAGAZINES

# CONTENTS

# ELSA

···»» Played by «‹···

## IDINA MENZEL

———

Gifted with amazing and powerful icy
abilities, Elsa faced a challenging journey
into adulthood but now reigns as Queen
of Arendelle.

01

## Who is Elsa?

The eldest sister in the kingdom's royal family, Elsa is the queen of Arendelle. She is reserved and poised, but also has an amazing power to create ice and snow.

## Childhood days:

Born with extraordinary abilities, as a child Elsa entertained her younger sister, Anna, by conjuring impressive ice displays – until, after creating a snowman the sisters called Olaf, Elsa accidentally injured her sister with her powers. From that day forward, Elsa was sequestered away, isolated from Anna and all of Arendelle, made to wear gloves and keep tight control of her powers. Elsa was all too aware how remaining remote from her sister would upset Anna, but she also was afraid of how dangerous her powers could be.

## As a young woman:

Years passed, and the distance between the sisters remained – despite Anna's attempts to bridge the divide – and even more so after their parents died in a shipwreck. The day of Elsa's coronation came, with the castle gates finally reopened, and the new Queen was shocked when Anna approached her and asked for her blessing to marry the visiting Prince Hans. Not wanting Anna to marry a man she'd only just met, Elsa refused. In the ensuing argument with her sister, Elsa lost control of her powers, revealing their existence to the terrified citizens and visiting guests alike, and plunging the realm into eternal winter. Elsa fled the castle and retreated to the North Mountain.

## Search and rescue:

Alone, Elsa embraced her powers and built a towering ice palace, as well as recreating Olaf and giving him life. She was content in her solitude, until she was sought out by Anna, with ice harvester Kristoff, his reindeer Sven, and Olaf in tow. When Anna apprised her of Arendelle's plight, Elsa, full of fear, again lost control of her powers, accidentally striking Anna in the heart.

## Elsa on the defense:

After summoning a gigantic snow creature, Marshmallow, to chase the group away, Elsa was attacked by Hans and a platoon of soldiers. Elsa was knocked unconscious and taken back to Arendelle where she was locked in the dungeon.

Charged with treason and due to be executed, Elsa used her powers to break free of her prison, but in the process caused a blizzard to engulf the kingdom. She was confronted by Hans, who told her that Anna had died of the ice wound Elsa inflicted. Devastated, Elsa collapsed, and the snow blizzard froze mid air. Hans was about to kill her when Anna appeared, throwing herself in front of his blade before completely freezing solid. Hugging her sister, Elsa mourned her loss, but was amazed when Anna began to thaw. As a result, the Queen realized that love was the key to ending Arendelle's winter. Now able to control her powers, Elsa reunited with her sister, and assumed her responsibilities as ruler of the kingdom.

## Into Frozen 2...

A few years later, Elsa begins hearing a strange voice calling her north, and senses that change is coming. After they are mysteriously pushed out of their kingdom, Elsa and her friends embark on a quest to an uncharted land in search of answers...

"Mythic characters are magical. But it's not aspirational, it's about the hard answers and truths that we face. There can be a tragic aspect, too, so in that way, they teach us about ourselves."
— Director/Writer/Chief Creative Officer, Jennifer Lee

02

**01.** Powerful Elsa faces a tough journey in *Frozen 2*  **02.** Concept sketch of Elsa

# Elsa's powers

"We realized there were lingering questions, and the biggest one was:
Why was Elsa born with magical powers?"
- Director/Writer/Chief Creative Officer, Jennifer Lee

## Idina Menzel, the voice of Elsa

03

*Frozen*'s Elsa is, without doubt, a tough, independent and powerful young woman — as much in terms of her personality as her magical ability to create and manipulate ice and snow. To play her required an actress who could not only deliver that film's show-stopping central number, "Let It Go," but who could also encompass the Snow Queen's profound fortitude. Idina Menzel was that actress.

On January 8, 2005, during her second-to-last performance of the *Wizard of Oz* spin-off musical *Wicked*, Menzel fractured a rib in an onstage accident. She was too hurt to play the leading role of Elphaba (which won her a Best Actress Tony Award) for what was supposed to be her final show. But to the delight of the Broadway audience, at the show's end Menzel appeared on stage in a red tracksuit and, despite her cracked rib, performed the closing number, "For Good." She received a five-minute standing ovation.

Menzel is one of America's most successful, beloved and enduring stage performers. She has, as a critic for the *Pittsburgh Post-Gazette* once wrote, "A voice that could be categorized as coquettish to flat-out belter and everything in between — and with a stage presence to match." As well as wowing audiences in *Wicked*, she also made a huge impression with her Broadway debut in 1996 as *Rent*'s Maureen Johnson, and earned a third Tony nomination as Elizabeth Vaughan in 2014 for the new musical *If/Then*. She is also the first Tony Award-winning actress to reach the Top 5 on the Billboard Hot 100 chart, which she achieved with the release of "Let It Go" in 2013.

Unsurprisingly, Menzel, the daughter of a therapist and a pajama salesman, wanted to be a performer for as long as she can remember. "I've been singing and acting and running around putting on shows in my living room since I was a little girl," she told the Roundabout Theatre Company last year. As a teenager in New York, when her friends were going to weekend parties, Menzel would

04

05

**03.** Idina Menzel provides the voice of Elsa (Photo: s_bukley / Shutterstock.com)

**04.** Elsa's powers start to evolve

**05.** Elsa meets some unusual inhabitants in the Enchanted Forest

be singing on stage at weddings or bar mitzvahs, honing those powerhouse vocals of hers.

Three decades later, she seems no less determined, and shows no sign of slowing down. She has reached a global audience in her role as Elsa, and the character is important to Menzel, not least in terms of her being an inspiration to girls and young women. She stands on her own two feet, and doesn't need a prince to save the day for her.

However, Menzel has confessed to feeling a little "uncomfortable" about this at times. "Everyone talks about me being a role model for young girls and that's not always the truth in my day-to-day personal life," she once told *The Telegraph* newspaper. "The older I get, I get wiser about some things, and yet I get more fragile and vulnerable about others." Though you'd never guess that from hearing her sing – whether she's belting out *Wicked*'s "Defying Gravity" or *Frozen*'s "Let It Go," Menzel's voice certainly sounds anything but fragile and vulnerable. ❄

# The Sisters

"[Mythic characters often] typically suffer a tragic fate - which might have happened to Elsa in the first film were it not for Anna..."
- Producer, Peter Del Vecho

# ANNA

...≫ *Played by* ≪...
## KRISTEN BELL

The quintessential fairy tale character, Anna is unflappable and an eternal optimist. But can there be a happily ever after when her home, sister, and friends face troubled times?

01

## Who is Anna?

Anna of Arendelle – sister of Elsa, and some might say the heart of the *Frozen* world.

## Childhood days:

Anna's early childhood was blissfully happy. She and her elder sister Elsa revelled in Elsa's abilities to create ice and snow, but everything changed when Elsa accidentally knocked Anna unconscious with her icy powers. The girls' parents, King Agnarr and Queen Iduna, took Anna to the mountain trolls, whose leader, Grand Pabbie, healed Anna and erased her memories of Elsa's powers. The King and Queen locked the castle gates, and Elsa was largely restricted to her bedroom, leaving Anna hurt and confused. As the years passed, the sisters grew ever more distant, compounded by the death of their parents in a shipwreck.

## As a young woman:

Three years later, Anna was excited when the castle gates were opened for Elsa's coronation. Finally, after many years, guests were visiting the castle, and Anna met Prince Hans of the Southern Isles. She fell for him and accepted his marriage proposal. But Elsa and Anna clashed over this, leading to Elsa accidentally plunging Arendelle into eternal winter before fleeing.

## New dangers:

Anna was determined to find her sister. Setting out on her own, she encountered an ice harvester named Kristoff and his reindeer, Sven. With Kristoff's help, Anna tracked Elsa to the North Mountain – on the way meeting Olaf, who had been unwittingly brought to life by Elsa's magic and where Elsa had created an ice palace refuge. But Elsa, upset by the news of the eternal winter she had created and consumed by fear, lost control of her powers again, accidentally striking Anna in the heart with an icy blast.

## True love

Kristoff took Anna to Grand Pabbie, who advised that Anna's heart had been frozen, and that only an act of true love would save her. Believing that a kiss from Hans was the answer, Kristoff and Anna returned to Arendelle, but it turned out that Hans' true intention was to take control of the kingdom. Anna was locked away, but Olaf soon came to the rescue, and Olaf helped Anna realize that Kristoff was her true love.

Anna escaped the castle and sought out Kristoff, but in her desperate attempt to find him, she saw Elsa collapsed on the ground about to be killed by Hans. Throwing herself in front of Hans' sword, Anna froze solid! A heartbroken Elsa hugged her sister, only to find that Anna began to thaw. The act of true love that Grand Pabbie spoke of was Anna's sacrifice. With the sisters' love for one another rekindled and Arendelle's winter ended, Anna punched Hans and reunited with Kristoff.

## Into Frozen 2...

When Arendelle is threatened, Elsa decides to venture to the Enchanted Forest beyond the kingdom in search of answers, and Anna is determined to accompany her. Having gained everything she ever wanted when she and her sister reunited, Anna will do everything she can to not lose Elsa again.

"For *Frozen 2*, we wondered what Anna would do now that she has everything she's ever wanted..."
— **Director/Writer/Chief Creative Officer, Jennifer Lee**

02

**01.** Princess Anna of Arendelle – the heart of the *Frozen* world  **02.** Concept sketch of Anna

# Anna's struggles

**Director/Writer/Chief Creative Officer Jennifer Lee on Anna:**
"Anna is the optimist. [A lot of] these characters are only human. They're not magical, but often enter into the dangers of a magical world. They go into the belly of the beast, suffering hardship and loss with great struggles - yet rise triumphant..."

03

"Anna had nothing to lose in the first movie - but now she has everything to lose because she got everything she ever wanted. While Elsa finds herself yearning for answers, Anna is trying to hang onto everybody and everything."

## - Director, Chris Buck

# Kristen Bell, the voice of Anna

Kristen Bell grew up watching Disney musicals – her favorites were *The Little Mermaid* and *Aladdin* – and like most young girls who grow up watching these movies, she fantasized about being a Disney princess. However, she had conditions. It had to be a "specific type of Disney princess."

*Frozen*'s Anna turned out to be the perfect role for Bell. She liked the way that, in the first film, the lonely princess of Arendelle talked with paintings and statues and spent a lot of time "bugging the staff" in her palace. "That's what made her so loveable to me," Bell said in an interview with *We Got This Covered* at the time of *Frozen*'s release.

It is fair to say that, so far, Bell's career as a leading screen actress has been as atypical as Anna is as a Disney princess. Despite being voted "Best Looking Girl" by her senior class on graduating high school in 1998, Bell never considered herself "pretty enough to play the pretty girl", and never fell into those kinds of roles. Her breakthrough was in the lead role of cult UPN teen-noir drama *Veronica Mars* in 2004, playing a high school girl investigating the death of her best friend. Veronica was something of a social outcast, and while Bell herself had a very happy high school life, she connected with Veronica's "scrappy" nature, and felt sympathy for her position. "I'm very quick to defend the underdog," she told *People* magazine in 2005.

This trait has come to define Bell in her work and life more than any other. It's not just about the kinds of roles she chooses, from the unhinged Elle Bishop in *Heroes* to the self-confessed "trash-bag" Eleanor Shellstrop in NBC sit-com *The Good Place*. She has, for example, heartily embraced nerd culture. She is a vocal fan of boardgames (in particular *Catan*, which she plays with her husband Dax Shepard), and has described the enthusiasts who attend events like Comic-Con as "the tastemakers of tomorrow." Nerdy, Bell maintains, "is the new cool."

She also refuses to play up to any image of celebrity perfection, being upfront, for example, about her own issues with depression and anxiety; "It's important for me to be candid about this so people in a similar situation can realize that they are not worthless," she said in May 2016. Furthermore, she is very active with charity work, helping to raise awareness of such issues as animal rights, prostate cancer, child poverty, Alzheimer's disease and global child hunger — this last concern even inspiring her to launch her own snack bar company, named This Saves Lives, whose proceeds go toward helping starving children.

If nothing else, Kristen Bell is a thoroughly empathetic person, and that is something she is determined to bear out through her work. She's not even keen on branding anyone a "villain." Which is another reason why *Frozen* so appealed to her: Anna's frost-weaving sister Elsa would, in most other movies, have simply been the bad guy. But, as Bell put it in a 2018 interview with *The Guardian*, "Not only does she not need to be forgiven for anything, she's the most sympathetic character in the whole piece."

Bell prefers her stories to be complex, replete with shades of gray, rather than swathed in black and white. So she makes sure her characters are complex, too, whether they're a high-school-reject detective, a "trash-bag" trying to learn ethics in the afterlife, or a Disney princess unlike any we've seen before. ✳

03. Anna faces danger in *Frozen 2*  04. Kristen Bell provides the voice of Anna (Photo Ga Fullner/Shutterstock.com)
05. Anna is stunned – and scared – by Elsa's new powers.

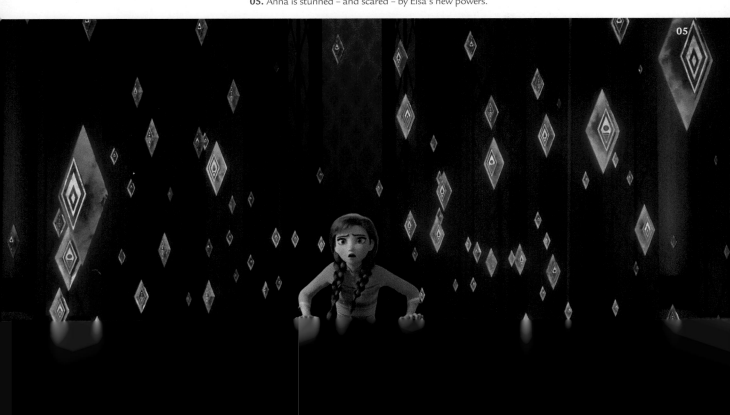

# KRISTOFF

## ·····》 Played by 《·····
## JONATHAN GROFF

———

Kristoff's heart was melted by Anna
in the first *Frozen* film, and now in *Frozen
2*, he is set to make a big decision about
their relationship.

01

## Who is Kristoff?

As a young, orphaned boy, Kristoff spent much of his time exploring the wilderness with his faithful companion, the reindeer Sven. Kristoff was fascinated by Arendelle's ice harvesters – watching and admiring them.

## First encounters:

One day, he witnessed the King and Queen of Arendelle riding with their daughters Anna and Elsa to Troll Valley to seek an audience with the trolls. Watching from afar, Kristoff was amazed to see Grand Pabbie, the trolls' leader, heal Anna – and then he was discovered by a female troll, Bulda. Bulda took a shine to Kristoff, and decided to adopt him.

## As a young man:

Many years later, now an established ice harvester, Kristoff encountered the grown-up Anna when he called at Wandering Oaken's Trading Post and Sauna, seeking supplies and carrots for Sven. The eternal winter set off by Elsa had driven up demand and prices for mountain gear, and when Kristoff accused Oaken of being a crook, he was thrown out of the store. Deciding to spend the night in a nearby barn, Kristoff was sought out by Anna, who bought him his supplies – and Sven his carrots – in return for taking her to the North Mountain in search of her estranged sister. En route, they also came across Olaf, the now-living snowman from Anna's childhood who had been given life by Elsa's powers.

## Danger zone:

The group found Elsa but were chased away and Anna was severely injured. Taking Anna to Troll Valley after noticing that her hair was beginning to turn white, Kristoff introduced her to his troll family, who tried to arrange a wedding for them! Kristoff learned from Grand Pabbie that the princess had been fatally wounded, and the only thing that could save her was an act of true love. Kristoff took Anna back to the castle and left her in the care of Prince Hans, even though Kristoff himself had fallen for her. Little did he know that Hans meant to let Anna die so that he could become ruler of Arendelle.

## True love:

Forced to return to Arendelle by a blizzard, Kristoff could only watch as Anna flung herself before Hans' sword to defend Elsa. Anna was frozen solid, leaving Kristoff bereft. Anna's act of true love in saving her sister thawed Anna. With the return of Summer to Arendelle, Kristoff was given a new sled by Anna, and bestowed the title of the kingdom's Official Ice Master and Deliverer, after which he and Anna shared a kiss.

## Into Frozen 2...

Now a permanent part of Anna's life, Kristoff decides it's time to take his relationship with Anna to the next level. Before he can, however, Arendelle is beset by a new threat, and Kristoff puts his proposal on hold in order to accompany Anna and Elsa on a dangerous journey to a mysterious land...

**01.** Kristoff's love for Anna takes him into dangerous territory  **02.** Kristoff and Sven, an inseparable duo

"Anna and Kristoff fell in love at the end of the first movie.
In *Frozen 2*, we get to see how their relationship evolves..."
- Producer, Peter Del Vecho

# Jonathan Groff, the voice of Kristoff

One of Jonathan Groff's earliest memories involves Disney Animation. He was, as a very young boy utterly smitten by *Snow White and the Seven Dwarfs*, the

revolutionary feature-length animation that put Disney on the cinematic map. Having seen it in a theater during a re-release run, he demanded to his mother they go straight back in and watch it again. She assured him they could always get it on video — though unfortunately at that time it was not available on home-entertainment formats. So she showed him *Sleeping Beauty* instead. Young Jonathan was not happy. "This is not *Snow White!*" he complained. "This is not what I remember seeing."

No doubt that's why Groff regards working on *Frozen* and *Frozen 2*, in the role of strapping, reindeer-impersonating mountain man Kristoff, as a dream come true. "I feel so lucky," he said at the time of the first film's release.

But it's not really a matter of luck. Groff was ideal for the role of Kristoff.

This was partly because during the audition process for the first film, it became clear his voice was the ideal match for Kristen Bell's as Anna. But mostly it was thanks to his lauded career on stage, particularly in musicals.

In 2006, just one year after earning his Actors' Equity Association card, Groff landed the lead role of Melchior Gabor in the Broadway rock musical *Spring Awakening*, for which he received a Tony nomination. In 2015, he received another Tony nomination for playing King George III in the smash-hit show *Hamilton*, as well as rave reviews ("Groff… finds new levels of comic brilliance in his short but convulsively funny appearances," wrote *Time Out New York*). Today, he might be better known for hard-hitting TV drama, playing determined FBI Special Agent Holden Ford in Netflix's true-life serial killer thriller *Mindhunter*, but the truth is: theatre is in Groff's blood.

Which does seem unlikely when you consider his background. Groff grew up in rural Pennsylvania, his mother a PE teacher, and his father a horse trainer. He spent much of his childhood on the family farm, playing in their fields, barns and horse stalls. Although, he wasn't exactly "country" in the traditional sense. His first-ever play was a home-made production of *The Wizard of Oz*, which he, his brother and their friends put on in his dad's barn. Groff, naturally, took the starring role: of Dorothy Gale. It was from that very moment he can trace his desire to be an actor. He was, at the time, only four or five years old. "My heart is always in musicals," he recently told the website *Absolute Music Chat*.

04

To Groff, working on a Disney movie is very similar to putting on a Broadway play, not just in the sense that it involves performance and singing, but also the way Disney workshops their scripts. "There's a lot of effort that goes into the story and character," he told *We Got This Covered*, citing the many changes that were made to Kristoff during the process of voicing him on the first film. He also thinks it was a wise decision to fill the *Frozen* voice cast with actors who have a theater background, like Idina Menzel (Elsa) and Josh Gad (Olaf). "I feel like this animated work lends itself well to the people who come from the theater," he said, "as there's a lot of improv."

It also clearly lends itself well to someone who, as a five-year-old, would joyously re-enact scenes from *Mary Poppins* in his bedroom, and who dressed up as Peter Pan for Halloween two years in a row. "You feel like you're a child at play when you're recording one of these [films]," he said. "That's what I strive for in every acting job.". ✳

**03.** Jonathan Groff. Kathy Hutchins / Shutterstock.com

**04.** Kristoff, the apple of Anna's eye

**05.** Sven and Kristoff speed into action!

05

# OLAF

## ···≫ Played by ≪···
## JOSH GAD

---

Created by Elsa several years ago, Olaf the snowman has now found a family with Elsa, Anna, Kristoff, and Sven the reindeer. His positive approach to life is invaluable in dark times.

01

## Who is Olaf?

A snowman magically brought to life, Olaf is a simple soul, innocent in the ways of the world. He's eager to find out all he can, and unhealthily obsessed with summer!

## Early days:

Olaf was first built by Elsa and Anna on that fateful night when Elsa accidentally injured her younger sister with her ice powers. Olaf was recreated by Elsa several years later, when she fled Arendelle after setting off eternal winter in the kingdom. Unafraid of her powers, Elsa made a new Olaf whilst creating her ice palace on the North Mountain – but this time, such was the strength of her abilities that Olaf was given life!

## New friends:

Olaf wandered the mountain, lost and alone, until he met Anna, Kristoff, and Sven in their quest to find Elsa. Recalling Olaf from her childhood, Anna provided a carrot for his nose – which Sven repeatedly attempted to eat – while Kristoff told him about their mission to return summer to Arendelle. Upon hearing this, Olaf exclaimed that he loved the idea of summer (much to the bemusement of Kristoff, who threatened to tell him what actually happens to snow in summer).

## New dangers:

Olaf led the group to the ice palace, but on arrival, Anna ended up being struck in the heart by a stray ice blast from Elsa. After learning that only an act of true love could save Anna's life, Olaf accompanied the group back to Arendelle, but became separated en route. Arriving at the castle, Olaf found Anna, locked in a room and dying, having been misled by the conniving Prince Hans. The snowman built a fire to keep her warm, and helped her realize that it was not Hans who is her true love, but Kristoff.

## A new Olaf:

Escaping from the castle, Olaf became separated from Anna in the blizzard; by the time he found her again, she was frozen solid, her last act having been to protect Elsa from Hans. But when Anna miraculously thawed, Olaf realized that the act of true love was Anna's sacrifice of herself for Elsa. In turn, this helped Elsa understand that love is the answer to controlling her powers, and she ended Arendelle's enforced winter, bringing back summer. Unfortunately, as a result, Olaf started to melt – until Elsa provided him with his very own snow cloud to sustain him. Smelling a flower, Olaf let out a sudden sneeze, blowing his carrot nose straight into Sven's mouth. Rather than eat it, however, Sven returned it to his new friend.

## Into Frozen 2...

Olaf has formed a strong bond with his family, and also developed a new perma-frost, thanks to Elsa's growing powers, which means he no longer needs his snow cloud flurry to enjoy living in Arendelle. When Elsa, Anna, Kristoff, and Sven embark on a quest to the Enchanted Forest, Olaf is excited to accompany his friends.

**01.** Olaf, *Frozen*'s resident snowman  **02.** Olaf with two of his besties – Kristoff and Sven  **03.** Olaf and Anna head into peril

# Josh Gad, the voice of Olaf

While most of his childhood friends laughed their heads off at the movies of Jim Carrey during the 1990s, Josh Gad was watching Charlie Chaplin. As a kid he became enraptured by the bowler-hatted comedy master of the silent era, and as a result, he's said, "I became obsessed with this idea of physical comedy."

Whether he's on the theater stage, TV, or the cinema screen, it's clear Chaplin's influence buried its roots deep, and Gad gives a trademark larger-than-life presence that energizes every scene he's in. Gad played the original Elder Cunningham in Broadway comedy-musical *The Book of Mormon*, for

example – a role that earned him a Tony nomination for Best Actor. In 2017, he brought us LeFou, the suffering sidekick to the villainous Gaston (Luke Evans) in Bill Condon's live-action retelling of Disney's *Beauty and the Beast*. And we can only imagine what Gad will do with the role of Mulch Diggums in the upcoming fantasy adventure *Artemis Fowl*, being a kleptomaniac dwarf who eats rock – and then weaponizes its explosive effect on his bowel…

Being such a physical actor and comedian, it might seem surprising that Gad has done so much voice-acting work over the years, in films like *Ice Age: Continental Drift*, *The Angry Birds Movie*, *A Dog's Purpose*, and of course the biggest animated movie of them all, *Frozen*. But Gad has never drawn a line between the physical and the vocal. "I'm sure if they ever released the footage of

me in the [*Frozen*] recording studio it would be very embarrassing," he admitted in an interview on CBC News in 2017, "because I flail around a lot. There was definitely a lot of physicality."

It is clear he feels a great affinity for his character, Olaf — after all, *Frozen 2* represents the seventh time he's voiced the cheery, optimistic living snowman. He's said he loves the way Olaf is so purely innocent and childlike, an ever-present reminder of sisters Anna and Elsa's childhood happiness together. "I got into this character by getting in touch with my inner child," he told CBC.

One of Gad's inspirations for the role was another very physical comedian, playing another iconic Disney animated character: Robin Williams as the Genie in 1992's *Aladdin*. "I remember sitting in the theater watching Robin Williams belt out his big number, 'You Ain't Never Had a Friend Like Me,' and I remember thinking to myself, 'I want to do that one day, that is my big dream,' said Gad during *Frozen*'s promotional campaign.

Like Williams in *Aladdin*, Gad ended up guiding the animation and character of Olaf far more than most actors do in movies like these. Early on in the production of *Frozen*, co-directors Jennifer Lee and Chris Buck invited him in to help with an animation test for the carrot-nosed snowman. They instructed him to just fool around, to try stuff out, on the understanding it wouldn't need to be used for the final film. However, said Gad, "that day is now the final version of Olaf's first scene in the movie." His fooling around became the rock-solid basis for the character.

Gad and Olaf, it seems, have become inseparable. Whatever else Gad does, whether it's working with Kenneth Branagh (on *Murder on the Orient Express* and *Artemis Fowl*), or appearing in Australian zombie comedy *Little Monsters*, to most of the world he will always be Olaf. Gad revealed (on *The Late Show With Steven Colbert* in 2017) that his own two daughters kept asking him to stop doing Olaf's voice when reading the *Frozen* book to them. But, as he jokingly pointed out, "It's my voice! I don't decipher between the two!" ✳

"Olaf is full of questions. He's contemplating life and death and existence - much like any kid would, but he's doing it the Olaf way!"
- Director/Writer/Chief Creative Officer, Jennifer Lee

**04.** The many movements of Olaf  **05.** The voice of Olaf, Josh Gad – Photo: Joe Seer/Shutterstock.com

# SUPPORTING CHARACTERS

## Queen Iduna

Wife to King Agnarr of Arendelle, and Elsa and Anna's mother. Queen Iduna's greatest joys were her two daughters, and she wished to be able to protect them from any dangers. But Elsa developed magical ice powers from a young age, and these grew – along with Elsa's questions. Iduna and Agnarr were forced to hide Elsa away for many years.

Several years later, after Iduna and Agnarr have been lost at sea, Anna comforts her sister Elsa by singing the lullaby their mother once sang to them.

**Played by** Evan Rachel Wood

Evan Rachel Wood started her performing career very young, appearing in the *American Gothic* TV series and then making her lead-role debut at the age of 11 with 1998's *Digging to China*. Her breakthrough role came in 2003's *Thirteen*, as a troublesome teen. More recently, Wood has become best known for playing the lead character, Dolores Abernathy, in HBO's *Westworld*, and of course for her role as Queen Iduna – a role that allows her to show off her singing skills. Wood formed an electro-pop act called Rebel and a Basketcase in 2016 and she now also performs as one half of the duo Evan + Zane.

## King Agnarr

The father to Elsa and Anna, and Iduna's husband. As we discover in *Frozen 2*, Agnarr headed to the Enchanted Forest when he was young with his father, King Runeard. Battle broke out between the Northuldra and the Arendellians, and Agnarr was saved in mysterious circumstances. King Agnarr and his Queen ruled as wise and benevolent monarchs until they were tragically lost at sea when their vessel was caught in a violent storm during a two-week ocean voyage.

**Played by** Alfred Molina

Molina's acting career started with a shortlived British sitcom in 1978 and then a brief but memorable role in *Raiders of the Lost Ark* in 1981. *Letter to Brezhnev* (1985) proved to be his breakthrough role. He focused on Hollywood roles from the mid-1990s and became an American citizen. Notable roles included *Boogie Nights* (1997), *Chocolat* (2000), *Spider-Man 2* as Dr Octopus (2004), and he starred in several TV and theater roles, including a Tony Award-winning lead performance in *Fiddler on the Roof* in 2004.

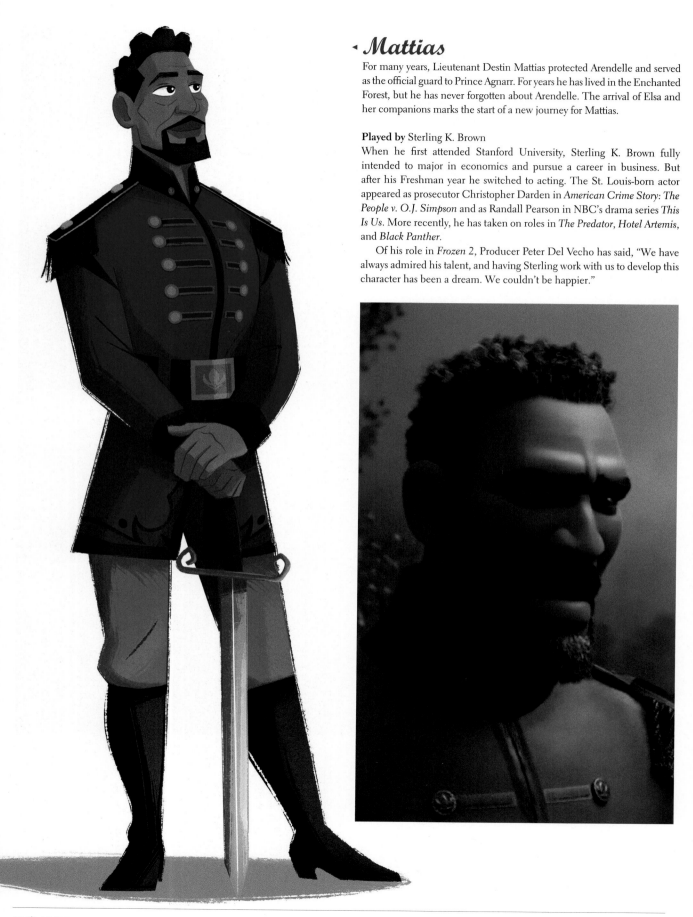

# Mattias

For many years, Lieutenant Destin Mattias protected Arendelle and served as the official guard to Prince Agnarr. For years he has lived in the Enchanted Forest, but he has never forgotten about Arendelle. The arrival of Elsa and her companions marks the start of a new journey for Mattias.

**Played by** Sterling K. Brown

When he first attended Stanford University, Sterling K. Brown fully intended to major in economics and pursue a career in business. But after his Freshman year he switched to acting. The St. Louis-born actor appeared as prosecutor Christopher Darden in *American Crime Story: The People v. O.J. Simpson* and as Randall Pearson in NBC's drama series *This Is Us*. More recently, he has taken on roles in *The Predator*, *Hotel Artemis*, and *Black Panther*.

Of his role in *Frozen 2*, Producer Peter Del Vecho has said, "We have always admired his talent, and having Sterling work with us to develop this character has been a dream. We couldn't be happier."

# Yelana ▸

Yelana is the unspoken leader of the Northuldra, a nomadic people who inhabit the Enchanted Forest. She is fiercely protective of her group and admires people who are willing to listen to nature.

**Played by** Martha Plimpton

Born in New York City to two actors, Martha Plimpton was destined for the big screen. She started off with a small role at the age of 10 (in 1981's *Rollover*) and went on to make a series of Calvin Klein commercials.

In 1985, Steven Spielberg cast her in *The Goonies*, followed by *The Mosquito Coast* in 1986, alongside River Phoenix with whom she also starred in the critically-acclaimed, *Running on Empty*.

# ◂ Honeymaren

Brave Honeymaren longs to leave the Enchanted Forest and explore the land beyond. When she meets Anna and Elsa, she wonders if they could be the key to her freedom.

**Played by** Rachel Matthews

Rachel Matthews came into the limelight when she starred in the horror movie *Happy Death Day*, in which her character is caught in a deathly time loop. The film was a hit and spawned a sequel two years later, *Happy Death Day 2U*, in which Matthews reprised her role. Matthews has also appeared in drama film *Ms. White Light*, TV mini-series *Looking for Alaska*, and comedy movie *Tankhouse*.

# Ryder ▸

Ryder is Honeymaren's brother and he likes to embrace life with gusto, handling tension with a disarming smile and a fun remark. Ryder has a love of reindeer, almost rivalling Kristoff's. Like his sister, Ryder yearns to explore the world outside the Enchanted Forest.

**Played by** Jason Ritter

The son of actor parents, Jason Ritter has appeared in several TV shows, movies, and theater productions. He first appeared on TV as a baby in *Three's Company* and would later find fame in the TV series *Joan of Arcadia*, going on to appear in many more TV shows, including *The Class*, *The Event*, *Parenthood*, *Us & Them*, *Girls*, *Kevin (Probably) Saves the World*, and *Quest*. Movie roles include *Freddy vs Jason*, *The Wicker Man*, and *7 Minutes*. ✳

# BEHIND THE SCENES

Making the world of *Frozen 2* takes the skill and dedication of a team of creators and artists whose efforts transport audiences to the magical land of Arendelle.

# CREATING *FROZEN 2*

Chris Buck (Director), Jennifer Lee
(Director/Writer/ Chief Creative Officer),
and Peter Del Vecho (Producer) reveal the
origins and themes of *Frozen 2*.

02

## WHEN DID YOU START WORKING ON *FROZEN 2*?

**Jennifer Lee (Director/Writer/Chief Creative Officer):** We started talking about it at the end of 2014. We didn't actually start working on the film then…

**Chris Buck (Director):** …But our brains were starting to churn… What would the next journey be? We fell in love again with those characters after doing the short animated film [*Frozen Fever*], so that inspired us.

**Peter Del Vecho (Producer):** The idea for a sequel came from Chris and Jen – they felt that there was more story to tell. The studio was happy that they were doing a sequel, but it had to come from the original filmmakers.

## WHAT WERE THE NEXT STEPS?

**PDV:** To create the sequel, we knew early on that the only way to do it is if we had our original team back, including the songwriters and the cast. That was a very important part of the decision.

**JL:** Yes – we (Lee and Buck) wanted to stay together, but we originally thought we were going to go off and do something very different. We got full support for that, so when we came back and said, "We've been thinking about *Frozen*," everyone was certainly happy. But this is why we've done so few sequels, because it really has to come from the filmmaker, fundamentally, and the original team's involvement was very important.

## WHAT OTHER FACTORS WERE INVOLVED IN BRINGING THE *FROZEN* CHARACTERS BACK?

**JL:** [Peter Del Vecho] had gone around the world doing some talks on *Frozen*, and came back and said he [had] a lot of feedback from people that Elsa resonated because she carries a lot of pressure on her shoulders. People who have high expectations on them feel a lot of pressure, but "Let It Go" set them free. Also, the question that kept coming was, "Why does she have powers?" That notion of responsibility that she carried – that we all carry – the weight of the world and the pressure she was feeling, they were emotionally enticing. And then there's the question of why [Elsa has powers] – the question we didn't even begin to ask before, because it was just enough that she was different.

**CB:** We were excited by the story, and also inspired by the fact that the fans had embraced these characters so much. We've got more story to tell, so we can't wait to tell it. We started talking about where we wanted to go. And that started to get their wheels turning.

## WHEN YOU CAME UP WITH THE MAIN IDEA FOR *FROZEN 2*, WERE THERE ANY OTHER IDEAS THAT YOU THOUGHT OF THAT WERE DISCARDED OR INCORPORATED INTO THIS?

**JL:** That's the whole process. There's so much that – as the editing department would say – is on the cutting room floor, but the essence of so many things we've tried have made

> ## "In both movies, we knew the ending. The path to get there was the difficult part."

their way in, in their own way. There's always this weird thing that happens. You look back to the beginning, and you can see all of the inspiration that led to where you are. But you can't believe what you made, because you didn't even know you could get there in the beginning (*laughs*). So there's this strange thing where the two feel very connected, as if it was always there all along, and yet the road to it, and what you end up with, is so much more complicated and bigger.

**PDV:** In both movies, we knew the ending. The path to get there was the difficult part.

**CB:** But the great thing about having that ending as your true north is that you know where you're going.

### WHAT KIND OF IDEAS DO YOU EXPLORE IN *FROZEN 2*?

**JL:** I think the big things for us were the concept of the magic of nature, and understanding Elsa's connection to that. One big story point came to light during a visit to a place we call the Epiphany Café – it was a small coffee area in one of the parliaments we visited in Norway [when we were researching locations]: we would have a story idea that affected Arendelle and nature, in the forest, in the past, and the connection between the two.

### WHY DO YOU THINK *FROZEN* IS SO SPECIAL TO FANS AND HAS SUCH A LASTING IMPACT?

**JL:** We're hearing a lot of stories, and every story is very different. The only thing that they have in common is that people have been able to project some part of themselves into one of our main characters, and it's spoken back to them.

**PDV:** It's definitely universal, because people relate to these characters all around the world. Part of it is, they're not perfect characters, they make mistakes, and that's part of what makes them relatable. They learn from their mistakes. Obviously, there's the music. Just the [*Frozen*] world alone – it's a believable world, [although] it's not a realistic world.

### WHO ARE YOUR FAVORITE *FROZEN* CHARACTERS?

**JL:** It's like choosing between your children. You can't! I have different moments of being proud of them, I have different moments where they drive me crazy, because they won't tell me the line I want them to tell me when I'm writing. But they are like family, so what I'm overwhelmed about is the opportunity to, A) get to work on *Frozen* to begin with, but B) to get to be with these characters again, and to grow with them. That is such an unusual thing to get to do, and so they feel alive to me. They feel real.

**CB:** To have favorites is tough, because there is so much of ourselves in each of these characters – there are personal stories that we've all shared that make it into these characters. So you see yourself in all these characters in certain ways. ❄

**01.** Elsa and Anna discover the mysterious monoliths

**02.** Anna looks on as Elsa uses her powers in the Enchanted Forest

**03.** Elsa, Anna, Kristoff, and Sven face more danger in *Frozen 2*

03

# MOTION & EMOTION

The *Frozen 2* animation team discuss the process and challenges of working on an animated movie – and the aspects that they enjoy the most.

01

02

03

## WHAT ARE THE VARIOUS STEPS IN MAKING AN ANIMATED FILM?

**Tony Smeed (Head of Animation):** As Heads of Animation, Becky and I work together to make sure that the animation that the directors want gets up onscreen.

**Becky Bresee (Head of Animation):** It's about the motion and emotion of the characters. So when the characters come into our department, [brought by] the supervisors of the characters – for instance, I supervised Anna on the first film, and Tony supervised Kristoff – the characters would be designed, and then go into Modeling. Then Animation would come in once Rigging was there, and then we got to play with the characters, to get them moving correctly and properly for who they were. On this film, we are overseeing those supervisors, helping to facilitate different things between the departments, and overseeing the Animation team.

## AND HOW DO YOU APPROACH PARTICULAR SCENES?

**BB:** What's fun is, for every sequence, we go into some "issuing" with the directors. Let's say it's the sequence of Charades [Elsa and Anna playing the game with Kristoff and Olaf]. The sequence will have been approved in [storyboards], moved on to Layout, which is the camerawork, and once those two things are done, it comes to Animation. So we have a good idea of what the story is behind the sequence, but in issuing, we get to hear [the Directors] Jen and Chris describe exactly what the scene should have in it to express what it's supposed to express on the big screen. A lot of times, animators get to play with how they're going to bring that. And that's part of the joy of our jobs.

**TS:** Yes – it might be something like, "I know this is what the character is saying, but this is how they're feeling. So even if they sound like they're happy, they're not – they're experiencing this." So that tells the animator that this sort of emotion has to come through. Jen and Chris are great about giving people their freedom to interpret.

**BB:** Even on some of the scenes that you think would be straightforward, like Anna walks into a room and stops and looks at Elsa, Jen would say, "Well, the reason that she walked into the room this way is because…" She knows these characters so well.

## WERE THERE ANY NEW TECHNIQUES/ TECHNOLOGIES AVAILABLE TO YOU ON THIS FILM?

**TS:** As technology advances, it meant that we had to essentially rebuild the characters. The good thing is that we are well

aware of the characters, we know what they're supposed to look like. We don't have to redesign them, but we do have to rebuild them and re-rig them.

**BB:** There are some things we learned on the first *Frozen* that, now that we got to rebuild them, we're saying, "Okay! We can make this easier for the animator if we do this." So it's not necessarily a bad thing that things had to be rebuilt. The challenge is trying to keep them looking and acting like themselves, as a through-line through production. We have a new render system for that.

> "It's actually fun for animators to have restrictions on the characters. It gives us a way to play with limitations."

**TS:** [The new program] Swoop was created for the sake of the Wind Spirit, Gale, character, to be able to draw arcs and paths to put Gale on, that we could quickly and easily edit. And that was a pretty big undertaking.

**BB:** Sometimes Gale would be represented by [dirt] clods blowing, or hair blowing, and in order for the tech animation artists to know what our intentions were as character animators, there was that invisible – or visible, when we were animating it –

ball-type thing to represent where Anna was [in relation to Gale].

**TS:** So if, let's say, we're animating Gale going [makes wind-swirling gesture] like that, we animate that and build it out, and the director said, "No, I want him to go up, make two loops, and then go out, and I want the timing to be more like this," he would [previously have to] rebuild everything from scratch. Whereas with Swoop, he can edit and build in another curve [without having to re-animate everything else around it].

### DO YOU HAVE ANY OTHER BIG, CHALLENGING CHARACTERS?

**BB:** We have Earth Giants. They're big moving characters, but they have restrictions. It's actually fun for animators to have restrictions on the characters. It gives us a way to play with limitations, which sometimes helps you find an interesting way to move.

### WHAT WERE YOUR FAVORITE CHARACTERS OR LOCATIONS TO ANIMATE, AND WHAT'S THE MOST CHALLENGING?

**TS:** There are a lot of deeply emotional aspects of the film. Just like the first one, there's a lot of humor, there's a lot of emotion, and there's a lot of depth as well. One of the most difficult things to do in animation is portray an emotion, without the aid of broad action, just being able to see how a character feels through the eyes and very subtle actions.

**BB:** And to get reactions from peers and from directors, just how it touches them, or it tickles them, is really the joy of our job. That's what we hope for. ✳

**01 & 02.**
Early *Frozen 2* sketches of Elsa and Anna

**03.** The Earth Giants provided a fun challenge for the animation team

# The Enchanted Forest

"The Enchanted Forest is filled with foliage, but underscored in magic. There are no blue skies in the Enchanted Forest. It is a beautiful place that's entirely surrounded by a wall of mist. There are deep layers of atmosphere that are filled with mystery..."
- Production Designer, Michael Giaimo

# FAIRY TALES

---

The *Frozen 2* story team discuss their approach to the new film and their favorite moments.

## HOW EARLY IN THE PROCESS DOES THE STORYBOARD DEPARTMENT COME INTO THE FILMMAKING PROCESS?

**Marc Smith (Director of Story):** We came in at different stages on this. I came in very early. At first, just the directors and the producer were involved, and then I came on probably around the same time as the Art Director. So that was around four years ago. There was really no script, just a lot of discussions at that point.

**Normand Lemay (Head of Story):** And you could say that was the core team. Especially with Marc coming in, it's these people that were talking to discuss the main ideas – what they wanted to do with the movie, where it should go, and trying to close some doors at some point, and start to invite more and more people in. The whole thing also comes down from the director's vision. In this case, one of our directors [Jennifer Lee] is also the writer. So a lot of it comes down from our two directors, which trickles down to us, and we have to first discuss the story that they want to tell, and try to accomplish their vision. But more often than not, we're seen as the first group that will attack, visually, the execution of the ideas.

**MS:** I often say it's a little bit of a misnomer – "Director and Head of Story," because it should really be more like "Director and Head of Storyboarding," which is slightly different. "Story" lives with the directors. It's their responsibility to come up with it. We are part of that, and we have long discussions, and we will have lots of opinions, but the responsibility for the story of the film falls on the directors.

## HOW CLOSELY DO YOU WORK WITH THE DIRECTORS?

**MS:** We work really close with them. Generally, the process is, once we have an idea of what the story is going to be and the script is starting to be written, we will talk with them about what is going to happen in the sequence, and either us or someone from our team will go and visualize a version of that, come back and show that to the directors, and then get their notes. In the next stage, it goes down to Editorial, where the directors look at it. Any changes they want to make, they kick back to the Story department. We go back, and we'll make those changes, until they sign off on it – "Okay, this is an approved sequence" – and then we do that over and over and over until we have the whole film, and we do more iterations. We do as much of that as we can, because we'll make the film between six and 12 times, adjusting the story, before we get it to hard animation. We will storyboard a sequence, so it will be individual drawings that represent scenes in the film. That goes to Editorial, where they make an animatic, and then the directors can watch it.

**NL:** Every sequence needs something different, its own amount of drawings, or even detail. We almost never [storyboard] just action. We always try to think about what's going on underneath the actions. So it's more storyboarding the thought process than an action.

**MS:** We really are basically storyboarding change. If Anna walks over and sits down next to Elsa, [it's] one drawing here, one drawing here. But if Anna walks to the couch but also looks out of the window and starts thinking about how beautiful the sky is – but she's worried that she left Kristoff somewhere – then all those little thought processes are going

to require changes and different drawings. So then it could be a hundred drawings.

## CAN YOU DISCUSS KEY STORYBOARD MOMENTS FOR *FROZEN 2* THAT YOU PARTICULARLY LIKED WORKING ON?

**NL:** For me, the "Into the Unknown" sequence is something great, because it's a song that comes in pretty early, and that works as an engine for the story. It's a key moment for Elsa, when she's going through the questions that are being raised within the story and within herself, that are going to have a big impact on the world of Arendelle, but also on a bigger stage. That sequence put everything into perspective and gives you

**01.** Elsa dives into danger in *Frozen 2*

**02-04** Elsa's powers – and character – develop throughout *Frozen 2*

an understanding of where she is in this film, after the first movie was complete. Where's her headspace at? She's singing it not necessarily to herself, but it's about her and her conflicts. It really helped us to storyboard anything else afterwards.

**MS:** The intention behind it when I was working on it, which got clearer when the other departments got involved – especially Effects – is that Elsa is not creating what she's seeing. She unleashes some of her powers, but it's this outside force playing with it that's showing her visions. Elsa at the edge of the ocean that was in the teaser [trailer] is one of the first things that we storyboarded on this, and that was a big goal, to feel like Elsa is not exactly the same person as she was in the first film; something has matured in her.

**NL:** She's not hiding, so at this point, she's definitely someone who has more experience and maturity.

**MS:** I feel like, thematically, we go a lot deeper in this film. Things test both of the women in ways that I'm really proud of. I'm glad we went for it as far as we did, because in the beginning, I was nervous about how far we were going to take them, and in the end, I think that's a thing that people are going to respond to.

**NL:** What I'm excited about is that it's not necessarily just a brand-new adventure, it's really part of a larger story that spans many years, generations, so it's a larger scope. And the scale, I would say, of this movie, is epic. I'm very excited to see it. ✳

# THE MUSIC OF FROZEN 2

Incredible animation, entertaining characters, dynamic action – *Frozen* is famous for many things. But one of the biggest things is its music.

T he same songwriting talents returned for *Frozen 2* – Kristen Anderson-Lopez and Robert Lopez. They created seven all-new original songs that capture the emotion, fun and intrigue of the storyline in a compelling way. The Lopezes credited their daughters for inspiring a lot of the music in the first film, and it seems that perhaps – in the words of the new *Frozen 2* song – some things never change...

"The girls – Anna and Elsa – are growing up," says Kristen Anderson-Lopez, "And our own girls are growing up, too. Our daughters are around the same age as [*Frozen 2* Director/Writer/Chief Creative Officer] Jennifer Lee's daughter. They informed the choices we made with *Frozen*, and have also informed the choices we made with *Frozen 2*. As the girls get more independent and have to walk their own paths and face their own moments of crisis without us there to protect them, it's ushered in a new era of parenting for us, which also made its way into the film."

Robert Lopez adds, "The epic tone of the new movie was something we wanted to hit right from the beginning. So, the lullaby, 'All Is Found,' which Queen Iduna sings to her young daughters, is meant to be a road map to the mythology of the story."

## ANIMATING THE MUSIC

**Becky Bresee (Head of Animation):** "My favorite [parts of the films] are always the songs. They're challenging, technically and emotionally. To be able to have a song come out of a character is tricky. Some mechanical and technical stuff happens when you sing. You try your hardest to make it believable, but if you push it too far into the physical, sometimes it doesn't work as emotionally as it could. I love musicals, I love singing, I love these characters, I love Disney musicals and fairytales. So to be a part of a film that has such epic songs and beautiful moments is really special."

**Tony Smead (Head of Animation):** "And the idea of having the songs is that the characters have no other alternative but to sing how they're feeling."

**BB:** "The brilliance of Kristen [Anderson-Lopez] and Robert Lopez is that they're able to weave – with the directors – the songs into the story to make it not feel like, 'Oh, okay, here's a song.'"

## The new songs of Frozen 2

**ALL IS FOUND (LULLABY) – sung by Iduna (also later sung by Anna and Elsa)**

**INTO THE UNKNOWN – sung by Elsa**

**SOME THINGS NEVER CHANGE – sung by the Cast**

**WHEN I AM OLDER – sung by Olaf**

**LOST IN THE WOODS – sung by Kristoff**

**SHOW YOURSELF – sung by Elsa**

**THE NEXT RIGHT THING – sung by Anna**

**THE PROCESS**

**Chris Buck (Director):** "[When the songwriters got involved], there wasn't a script yet, there was just the idea. We had many conversations about what the music could be and what some of the songs could be, very early on."

# Songs

## All Is Found (Lullaby)

Iduna is very close with her daughters, and shares an important – though mysterious – lesson through a song entitled "All Is Found." The haunting lullaby is about a river that holds all of the answers.

Evan Rachel Wood was cast as the voice of Queen Iduna. "There was something about Evan's voice that we really zeroed in on," says Producer Peter Del Vecho. "Her voice sounds like there's something underneath it – something hidden from the past..."

## Into The Unknown

In the early stages of the film, Elsa is being beckoned by a voice from far away. She initially tries to ignore it, but the calling is strong and becomes irresistible, as reflected in the original song "Into the Unknown." Elsa learns that answers await her – but she must venture far from home to receive them. As Elsa sings, her powers reveal themselves in new ways, creating life-like landscapes and creatures...

# Some Things Never Change

The cast's positive spirit is reflected in a song that begins in an effort to appease Olaf's uncertainty about the ever-evolving world around him. The song, "Some Things Never Change" – featuring Anna, Kristoff, Elsa and Olaf – introduces the idea of change to the story – changes in the weather and in appearances. But some things – like the love for friends and family – are constant.

## When I Am Older

As the epic adventure gets underway, the friends find themselves in the Enchanted Forest and Olaf faces a series of inexplicable events, illustrated in the song "When I Am Older." Despite the mystery and dangerous realities coming to life before his eyes, the lovable snowman is convinced that one day, it will all make sense.

## Lost In The Woods

Alone in the Enchanted Forest, Kristoff sings to calm himself and face his insecurities, as well as imagine the possibility of a life without Anna. For the first time in his life, he feels lost.

# Unanswered questions

"We felt there were unanswered questions about Elsa and Anna's parents and where their ship was going when it went down."
- Director/Writer/Chief Creative Officer, Jennifer Lee

# DESIGNING AN EPIC

---

*Frozen 2* is full of character moments and exciting events, but the scenery and look of the film is essential in bringing the story to life.

## WHAT IS THE PROCESS FOR CREATING THE PRODUCTION ART FOR *FROZEN 2*?

**Lisa Keene (Co-production Designer):** Usually, we start after getting a treatment or a script, and then things that haven't already developed have to be realized and visually developed. Once those get approvals, then we move into producing those pieces of art.

**David Womersley (Art Director Environments):** [At the beginning, in terms of design and visual development, we had about maybe seven people, including us.

**LK:** We're the first ones in. We started at the beginning, and we went all the way through to the end. But in terms of the creation of one of these films, [the number of people working on it altogether] is enormous. Visual Development happens in there, too. So there will be a script that goes to the Storyboard department, and then we get to go play! We get to go do blue sky from that.

**DW:** The two of us are very back and forth – we have to be, because we have to cover for a lot of things. We have to create a lot of artwork so that we can show it to the directors, and to Mike Giaimo, our Production Designer, and get some kind of direction, so that when the other staff come on, we know which direction we're going in at that point, so we have a lot more confidence in bringing them on.

## HOW DO YOU FACTOR IN NEW ARTISTS THAT JOIN THE TEAM?

**DW:** A certain artist may get to [work] on a certain story location, because they might have a proclivity for that kind of artwork, or that kind of place and that kind of design. You do tend to find that certain people do tend to get certain things, and they get to take a location quite a ways down, to the point that we could start modeling the locations.

**LK:** It has more to do with casting a particular artist who does something to their skillset the best than it does, say, location. For instance, between us, David really likes structures and

## "I'd use the word 'epic' for this film. Epically magical."

buildings, and things that are more architecturally oriented. I tend to like things that are more organic. We make a great team, because we're covered on both sides.

**DW:** I pretty much focus on environments and the sets. I always say that, if it breathes, I don't deal with it – unless it's a tree, because trees breathe! (*laughs*)

**LK:** I don't do characters myself. We have a Supervisor or Art Director of Character that handles all of that, who works very closely with Mike Giaimo, who specializes in that side of things. I touch a lot of different things. I work with Effects pretty closely, working on the way something might look, and then I track with them. I also work with the lighters, so for a lot of the work that I do, I work on all the color scripts and all of the visual kind of color narration for the film. I work that out with the directors, and then I track that all the way through Lighting.

## HOW DOES THE VISUAL LANGUAGE OF THE NEW FILM COMPARE TO THE WORLD CREATED FOR THE FIRST *FROZEN*?

**DW:** We obviously had a lot based not just on the first movie, but also from some shorts that we had done. Those gave us various things that we could start with, so we weren't starting from scratch, but that was really just for the Arendelle section of the movie. Obviously, it's a travel movie, so they go somewhere else. The forest itself and all those other places the characters go to were all created from scratch.

## ARENDELLE LOOKS A LITTLE DIFFERENT IN THIS FILM WITH THE MORE AUTUMNAL COLORS. HOW DID YOU APPROACH THAT?

**DW:** When buildings are covered in snow, it creates a specific graphic look with cool colors. Some of the buildings were originally designed to look good against snow and ice. Not only did we have to remove the snow from those we wanted to reuse, we had to adjust them to look good against a new backdrop that included not just trees and leaves, but fall decorations.

## HOW DO YOU DECIDE WHAT NEEDS TO BE VISUALIZED?

**LK:** When you read a script, it has emotions. Color carries emotion. My job is to sit down with the directors and [Production Designer] Michael Giaimo, and figure out what the narrative is that we're telling. What do we want our audience to feel all the way through the film? And so for every sequence, every shot, and every scene, we work all those color arcs out, so that we can actually see a graph, and we can make sure that the graph is arcing correctly emotionally to the story. Not only does that work from shot to shot, but the characters have to go through their color arcs, too – so there's another whole layer to those color scripts. We start with an emotional arc of color scripting, and then we go into color keys. Once the color script is approved, we take those colors and actually apply them to a finished scene. So then that's what happens in lighting – we take all those color arcs all the way through. It's a way of everybody holding hands and agreeing to what we want our movie to look like, with color first, so that there are no surprises later on.

**DW:** We also have a shape language. In fact, when we were doing the castle, and the village, and the fjords, we exaggerated both the vertical and the horizontal. We took anything that seemed like it was too boxy and square and, because of what we've seen on our trips [for location research, to Norway, Finland and Iceland], there was an exaggeration. It was either this way [vertically] or that way [horizontally]. We decided to exaggerate horizontally or vertically. You don't see many squares in our movies.

**LK:** Yes. If there's a table in a room, it's been stretched out [to be rectangular].

## CAN YOU DISCUSS ANY KEY VISUAL MOMENTS YOU ESPECIALLY LIKED WORKING ON?

**LK:** Oh, my gosh. It's big and it's epic and it's full of beautiful magic and it's a sweeping story.

**DW:** I'd use the word "epic" for this film. Epically magical. ✳

**01.** Anna faces an emotional time, reflected in her environment

**02.** Detailed Production Design background art from *Frozen 2*

**03.** A bird's-eye view of Arendelle

# A mythic character

"We realized that in the first movie, we unknowingly had both a myth and a fairy tale going on at the same time. Elsa was definitely a mythic character, a type of character which generally carries the weight of the world on their shoulders and does things the rest of us can't."
- Producer, Peter Del Vecho

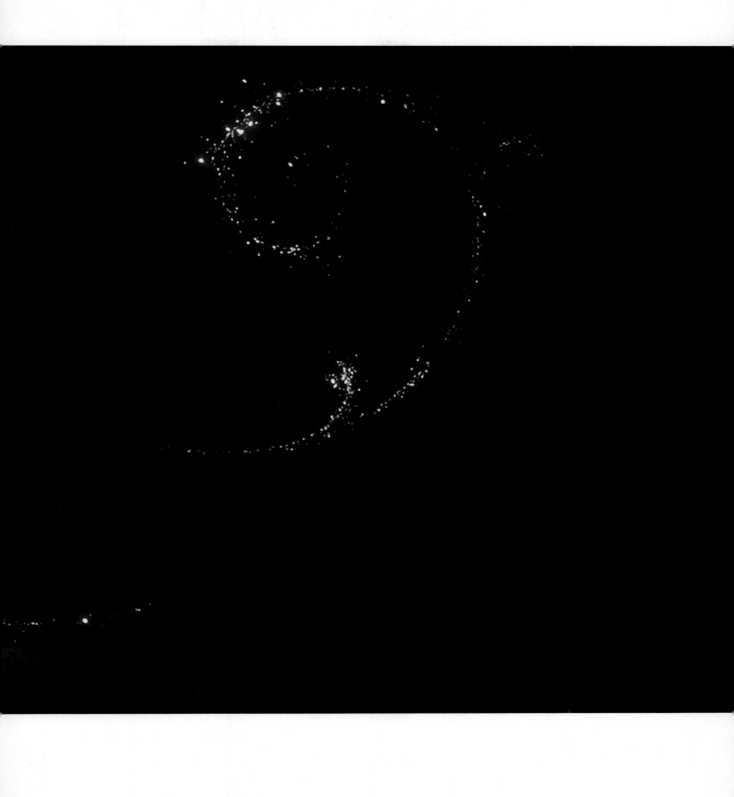

# MAKING MAGIC

---

The *Frozen 2* Effects team are there to add
that extra touch of magic to the movie.

## WHAT WERE THE MOST CHALLENGING EFFECTS FOR *FROZEN 2*? HOW DID YOU CREATE THEM?

**Erin Ramos (Effects Supervisor):** Water is always a difficult thing to tackle, because there are so many moving pieces involved. It's not just the water, it's everything that goes on top of it. Also, there's so much interaction between the water and our effects animation that we have to go back and forth with the different teams to make sure we get the performance that we want.

**Dale Mayega (Head of Effects Animation):** [In *Frozen*], Elsa runs across the fjord and freezes that, and that was a lot simpler, because it was a level surface. In this case, she's running on the ocean, and the ocean is constantly changing, so we had to work with the character animators to have everything working at the same [pace]. We had an effects designer on our team, who pitched some ideas in terms of how that ramp of ice is formed.

Originally, we had some ideas where we were freezing the actual wave as it's cresting, but then we wanted to have something more designed. That's when we pitched this idea of Elsa forming this ice ramp, so there was a lot of choreography in terms of exactly when the ice ramp would form, and what the surface is that she's running on.

**Marlon West (Head of Effects Animation):** We wanted to have the effects in this film track things that Elsa had already done in the past, and also be supportive of who she is as a person now. There was a lot of involuntary magic and almost accidental things that she did in the first film. When we meet her in this film, she's in full control. Everything she makes is much more powerful and effortless.

## WHAT WOULD YOU SAY THE BIGGEST "WOW" EFFECTS MOMENT IS IN *FROZEN 2*?

**ER:** When you watch this movie you're going to realize how effects-heavy it is, and how diverse the effects are. For me, every sequence was a "wow" moment.

**DM:** Each shot is so choreographed and art-directed. In fact, every time that Elsa does some magic, it's different.

## WHAT ARE SOME OF YOUR FAVORITE SCENES IN THE FILM, AND HOW DID YOU TACKLE THEM?

**MW:** Elsa's interaction with the Nokk [the water horse] is one of my favorite moments in the film, because you have a completely mythical creature that exists underwater and above water, it has to behave like people expect a horse to behave but it has to also be made of water, so we have to be supportive of the animation performance, because the team had animated a horse. We were careful to support the storytelling and the character performance. We needed to make that character look like a horse – make its mane and its tail behave like water, as well as actually having the water that drips off of the mane and the tail behave like physical water

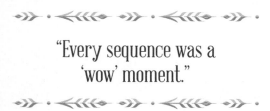

"Every sequence was a 'wow' moment."

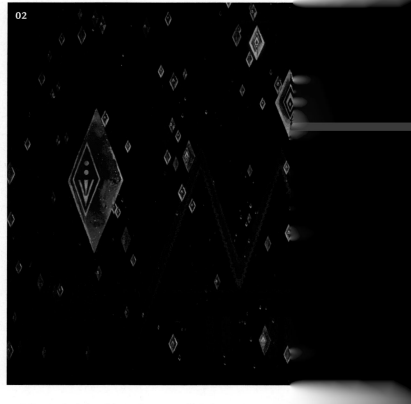

02

It has to be believable to the viewer, but also can't step on the performance of the character animation. The ocean itself has to behave like water, and we don't try to make utterly realistic water – we're going for something that's believable in the context of *Frozen*. We have this creature that has to be made of water, and can interact with this surface.

**DM:** We did an earlier test for [the Nokk] where we were trying to treat it more like real water, and some of the things that we were finding were that if we had too much real water, then we wouldn't be able to maintain the performance.

**ER:** When the water horse is underwater, what does that look like? Because what does water look like when it's in the water? It looks like water (*laughs*). So we worked closely with the art directors. I think we made something that looked pretty magic.

**MW:** We did some research and we found some underwater volcanic venting, and we used that to create the mane, so it felt more gaseous. We make things that are completely artificial, but we always look for things from the natural world to root these fanciful creatures and fanciful effects into.

## WHAT ARE THE MAJOR CHANGES IN TECHNOLOGY BETWEEN THE FIRST FILM AND THIS FILM?

**ER:** We had to animate this environment, and so we had to build a whole new [way to do that]. The Environments team were jiggling all the berries, and kicking up the leaves, and the trees are moving.

**DM:** The forest needed to be natural. We set up a workflow to enable us to animate anything happening in the environment.

**ER:** You notice the wind, the trees are slightly blowing all the time, the grass is moving underneath the characters' feet. It's those little things that make the movie really special. ✳

**01.** Elsa's incredible ice ramp

**02.** Anna is surprised by falling crystals

**03.** The magical Water Nokk presented some interesting challenges for the Effects team

# After happily ever after

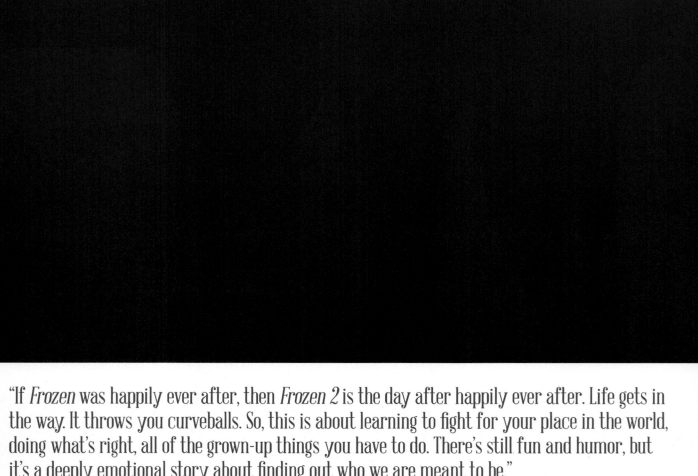

"If *Frozen* was happily ever after, then *Frozen 2* is the day after happily ever after. Life gets in the way. It throws you curveballs. So, this is about learning to fight for your place in the world, doing what's right, all of the grown-up things you have to do. There's still fun and humor, but it's a deeply emotional story about finding out who we are meant to be."
- Director/Writer/Chief Creative Officer, Jennifer Lee

# THE COLORS OF
# *FROZEN 2*

For *Frozen 2*, the crew looked beneath
the snow and ice to uncover
an unexpected palette.

02

## "A fall palette means an incredibly vibrant environment with striking colors" - Production Designer, Michael Giaimo

Before working on *Frozen 2*, some of the crew headed off on a research trip to the Nordics to get ideas for the look of the new film. Production Designer Michael Giaimo, Directors Chris Buck and Jennifer Lee, Producer Peter Del Vecho, Director of Story Marc Smith, and VP of Creative Development Jessica Julius headed out on a trip to Norway, Finland, and Iceland to study the landscapes and the cultures there. The *Frozen 2* team spoke to historians, experts in the local customs and cultures, and environmental authorities and botanists.

The trip took place towards the end of the year, so the team could get inspiration for the autumnal palette of *Frozen 2*, as Production Designer Michael Giaimo explains: "Anna and Elsa go on very specific journeys in *Frozen 2*, and they both grow and mature in the process. Little by little they each peel back layers, revealing more and more depth and dimension in these characters. For me, that meant removing the layers of snow and getting down into the earth.

"A fall palette means an incredibly vibrant environment with striking colors, and I was initially concerned that it would pull focus from our characters or look like a new place and time. But we were able to create a *Frozen* version of Fall that still felt cool. We minimized the yellows in favor of oranges, orange-reds and red-violets. It's distinctive to our world.

"The height of the trees is incredible – and that works so beautifully in the *Frozen* language, which is based on verticality. It was truly striking." ✳

03

04

# FROZEN 2 FASHIONS

The film's creators talk us
through all of the latest looks
in the new movie!

01

"She's still Elsa, she's still *Frozen*, but she's got a
little bit of warmth."

## *Elsa*

**Brittney Lee (Visual Development Artist):**
For Elsa's nightgown (left), [Production Designer] Mike
[Giaimo] wanted initially to skew a little bit warmer, but
anything that we tried was too warm for her, post-"Let It
Go." So it's an ombre, more red on top and more blue on the
bottom, to hint there's this ice on the base of the nightgown,
and she's still Elsa, she's still *Frozen*, but she's got a little bit of
warmth to hopefully reflect the warmth of the environment
that she's in with her family.

Whatever Elsa was wearing needed to reflect her ability
to go through a lot of different [environments]. We had to lift

her hemline off the floor, and that's something we'd never
done with her. In a way, it breaks what we know her silhouette
to be. We had a hard time trying to lift her coat, while at the
same time preserving some amount of her ethereal qualities.
We tried to do that by tailoring the coat and making the capes
on the back hearken back to the Snow Queen, but it was
definitely a challenge.

The boots made of ice were more of a no-brainer. Elsa
needed to have a little bit of elevation and, obviously, she would
make these boots out of ice, so that was less difficult, once we all
agreed and said, "Yeah, we've got to lift this hemline."

**01/02/03.**
Experimenting
with Elsa's
*Frozen 2* outfits.
Concept art by
Brittany Lee

04

> "Anna has a completely new hairstyle. We let her hair down."

05

06

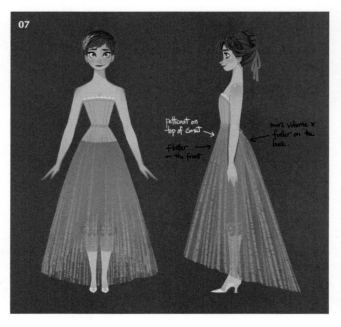

07

**04.** Early costume sketches for Anna

**05.** More defined Anna costume art

**06.** Experimenting with styles

## *Anna*

**GSL:** Anna has a completely new hairstyle. We let her hair down. We're trying to show that she is three years older. When we had the two braids on the side, that is iconic of Anna, [but] it makes her look young. Once we started putting her hair down, she suddenly looked right, but we have two braids – like an infinity braid.

08

09

10

**07/08/09.** More advanced art showing Anna's dresses

**10.** Kristoff and Anna adopt "couples outfits" in *Frozen 2*

## *Kristoff*

**GSL:** Britt designed Kristoff's costume. Now Kristoff and Anna are a couple, so they're wearing couples outfits (*laughs*). They are color-coordinated, but not matchy-matchy. I just love the couples look.

**BL:** They're not quite matching – but they compliment. We kept Kristoff's silhouette, for the most part, and updated his materials. His sash, which was originally more traditionally Norwegian graphic design-based, has the Arendelle wheat pattern on it, to signify that he's at home in Arendelle, but he's still his mountain man self. Sven's [harness] has the wheat pattern, too.

**11.** Mattias' style

**12.** Mattias in *Frozen 2*

**13.** Mattias and his men meet Anna in the Enchanted Forest

11

# *Mattias*

**GSL:** Mattias is one of the new characters. When we see Mattias again now, 30 years later, the outfit is weathered, so you feel time has passed since the first time you saw him.

**BL:** For Mattias, we had a bit of established designs for the Arendelle Royal Guard from the first *Frozen*, so his costume was based on that. Originally, Mike [Giaimo] asked me to look at uniforms from the [mid-19th-Century] Italian guard, some of which had over-the-shoulder capes slung very elegantly. We also looked at Norwegian designs.

## *Iduna*

**BL:** Iduna was one of the last characters that we designed on the first film, so we had very little time to run that costume through the entire pipeline. That was one of the first things that we revisited. We changed some materials – we changed some silks to something like linen that felt like it was cozier on her – something the [young princesses] would want to snuggle with. But the main design stayed the same.

**GSL:** There are more shimmers in her fabric, and the embroidery looks gorgeous. We use real fabric as reference, to see how it moves and how it feels, and then we stylize it.

**BL:** Yes – if we were to one-to-one directly take a fabric and implement it, it would look out of scale and out of place. ✳

**14/15/16.** Queen Iduna's look is "something the princesses would want to snuggle with"

# FREEZE FRAME!

## 20 *FROZEN* EASTER EGGS

---

Keen eyes might be able to spot these
Easter eggs and inside jokes from the first
*Frozen* movie...

# FROZEN

· Release / November 19, 2013
· Directors / Chris Buck and Jennifer Lee
· The highest grossing animated film of all time

**1** Rapunzel and Flynn Rider from *Tangled* (2010) can be seen attending Elsa's coronation.

**2** Concept art from Walt Disney Pictures' *Tangled* appears as a painting during the song "For the First Time in Forever."

**3** The painting was also inspired by *The Swing* (1767) by Jean-Honoré Fragonard.

**4** Anna eats candies originally seen as part of the scenery in the Sugar Rush game from *Wreck-It Ralph* (2012).

**5** A Mickey Mouse doll is half-hidden on a shelf in Oaken's Trading Post.

**6** One of Anna's favorite phrases – "Wait, what?" – was added to the script compliments of Kristen Bell.

**7** Hans' horse, who keeps Anna from falling in the water before the coronation, has a name: Sitron, which means "lemon" in Norwegian.

**8** During Olaf's sing-along, his dance with four seagulls is a visual nod to Bert's dance with four penguins from *Mary Poppins* (1964).

**9** Olaf's sing-along includes a visual reference to the Coppertone sunscreen baby.

**10** Joan of Arc is among the paintings seen during the song, "For the First Time in Forever."

**11** Another one of the paintings in *Frozen* resembles Elizabeth and Mr. Darcy as seen in the 1995 BBC miniseries *Pride and Prejudice*.

**12** A painting in Anna and Elsa's castle can also be found in Fred's Mansion from *Big Hero 6* (2014).

**13** Filmmakers invited a real-life reindeer into the Walt Disney Animation Studios, observing the animal's physical makeup and mannerisms, which were later caricatured in the making of Kristoff's reindeer buddy Sven.

**14** In an effort to perfect Elsa's icy magic, filmmakers called on Dr. Thomas Painter, a scientist from the Jet Propulsion Laboratory in Pasadena – known as "Dr. Snow" – to learn about snowflakes from a molecular level.

**15** Rosemaling, a style of decorative folk art found throughout Norway's history, appears throughout the film – on clothing and within the architecture. It is even evoked in Elsa's magic and her icy creations.

**16** The symbol of Arendelle can be seen on plates in the bakery scene in *Zootopia* (2016).

**17** During the song "In Summer," there are two hidden outlines of Olaf's body: one in his drink cup formed by ice cubes, and one formed by the clouds in the sky when he's lying on the picnic blanket.

**18** Hans appears on a "Wanted" poster in the police station of *Big Hero 6* (2014).

**19** There are two references to the TV Show *Arrested Development*: One is when Hans and Anna are talking and they say dialogue from the show: "We finish each other's..." – "Sandwiches!"

**20** And the second *Arrested Development* reference: the Duke of Weselton performs the Chicken Dance at the Coronation Ball, as popularized on the show.

# THE FROZEN PHENOMENON

A look at why the first *Frozen* movie was so successful and why the franchise continues to capture the imaginations of fans around the world.

**W**hen *Frozen* was originally released on November 27, 2013, it was clear from the get-go that the film was going to be a smash hit. Disney had been promoting the movie for months, releasing the first trailer – featuring Olaf and Sven battling good-naturedly over Olaf's carrot nose – in June, and previewing the songs "Let It Go" and "In Summer" at the D23 Expo in August. But few could have predicted the phenomenon that *Frozen* became. Apart from its gargantuan global box office – it took over $1.2 billion at cinemas worldwide, making it the most successful animated movie ever at that time – the film resonated with an audience of all ages in a way that happens once in a generation, achieving a ubiquity via toys, books, costumes, accessories, parties, and, of course, DVD and downloads, played on endless repeat in millions of households.

On the surface, *Frozen* is a fairly straightforward story. Based on Hans Christian Andersen's 1844 fairy tale *The Snow Queen*, it follows two sisters, Anna and Elsa, the latter heir to the throne of Arendelle and possessing terrifying icy powers. When Elsa loses control of her abilities and engulfs the kingdom in seemingly eternal winter, Anna sets out on a quest to save both her sister and Arendelle, aided by ice harvester Kristoff, his reindeer Sven, and Olaf, a comical snowman brought to life by Elsa's abilities.

That simple plot belies how extraordinary – revolutionary, even – *Frozen* actually is. Unlike previous Disney films – in which, typically, any romance is between a handsome prince and a fair maiden – in *Frozen*, the love at the heart of the movie is that between Anna and Elsa: two sisters whom fate has driven a wedge between, and who must overcome adversity and circumstance in order to rediscover the sororal love they had as children. Conversely, the handsome prince of the piece – Prince Hans, whom Anna falls head-over-heels in love with

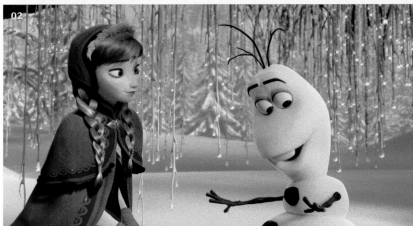

04

As prevalent as the toys and tie-ins were, however – indeed, still are – the craze for merchandise was merely a symptom of the audience's connection with the film. *Frozen* spoke to a generation of children. Kids connected with the film on a deep level, especially with its theme of empowerment, of embracing your feelings rather than repressing them. The sequence where Elsa, unleashed from the constraints of duty and society, finally gives free rein to her abilities and conjures her ice-palace refuge, is undeniably powerful, helped in no small art by the epic nature of the accompanying "Let It Go."

Then there's the relationship between the sisters – shattered after Elsa accidentally injures Anna at a young age, then plunged into a deep freeze both by the death of their parents, and by Elsa's need to keep her distance and suppress her powers. The sisters' travails speak not only to anyone who has a sibling, but to everyone who has ever had a fractured friendship of some kind. As the film's title suggests, Anna and Elsa's love for one another is literally frozen, only to be thawed by film's end thanks to Anna's selfless sacrifice.

Not that it's all so serious. Part of the charm of *Frozen* is its humor, personified by Olaf, the naive snowman obsessed with summer. Along with Sven and Kristoff, Olaf forms a comedy trio that injects regular jokes into the heightened drama. The frosting on the cake is the sweet relationship between Kristoff and Anna, who latterly realizes that it's the humble ice harvester rather than the superficially charming Hans who is her true love.

Trying to quantify why *Frozen* has become such a phenomenon is like trying to capture a snowflake. You can point to the story, the characters, the songs, the fact that the film has two strong female leads, and any number of other factors besides. In truth, it's because of all of these things, plus that indefinable extra something that lifts a film from being merely a hit to a

– turns out to be a conniving scoundrel, only interested in the princess as a way of gaining control of Arendelle.

Just as vital as the atypical story, however, are the characters, the songs, and the animation. Each of the protagonists is remarkably well defined, with Anna and Elsa particularly complex creations – the former exuberant, flighty, but confused and hurt by her sister's apparent rejection of her; the latter aloof, reserved, consumed by her struggle to contain her dangerous powers. Beyond the show-stopping "Let It Go," the soundtrack boasts songs that sear themselves into the memory, from the sweeping "For the First Time in Forever" to Kristoff's gentle ditty "Reindeer(s) Are Better than People." As for the animation, art director Michael Giaimo and his team built on the style established in 2010's *Tangled*, blending CGI and hand-drawn animation to brilliant effect.

The story; the characters; the songs; the animation: all of these combined to strike a chord with the audience. In the weeks and months following the film's release, *Frozen* became an ubiquitous presence. Anyone attending a children's party in the wake of the film will have noted the preponderance of Anna and Elsa costumes, girls responding to Anna's exuberance and bravery and Elsa's cool, calm and collected nature. Before long, *Frozen*-themed kids' parties became de rigueur. Sing-a-long screenings of the film packed out movie theaters, while in 2014 alone, the soundtrack sold 10 million copies worldwide. From live shows to musicals, lunch boxes to dolls, *Frozen* was everywhere.

*Frozen*'s timeless themes of love, family, and friendship have earned it a place in the hearts of millions, children and adults alike.

**01.** Elsa, a heroine for our times

**02.** Anna and Olaf

**03.** Prince Hans greets Anna

**04.** Kristoff and Sven, his faithful reindeer

cultural event. *Frozen* is the sum of its parts and more. It has enchanted legions of fans the world over – including children who know every word of every song, who can reenact any scene of the film – given rise to mountains of merchandise, a Broadway musical, two short films, and now, at last, in the shape of *Frozen 2*, a feature-length sequel.

The true magic of *Frozen* is that, for whatever reason, it has transcended its cinematic origins to become a whole world unto itself. Anna, Elsa, Olaf, Kristoff, Olaf, and Sven have become as recognizable to fans as Disney's other icons The film's timeless themes of love, family, and friendship have earned it a place in the hearts of millions, children and adults alike.

Now, with *Frozen 2*, that love is set to be rekindled, as well as lit anew in the hearts of millions more. The phenomenon that is *Frozen* shows no signs of stopping its snowballing popularity any time soon. ✳

"In the end, *Frozen* and *Frozen 2* work together to form one complete story."
– Director, Chris Buck

# DISNEY LIBRARY

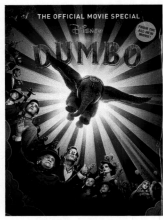

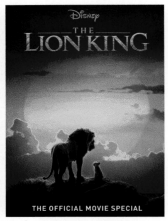

**DISNEY** *DUMBO*
THE OFFICIAL MOVIE SPECIAL

**DISNEY•PIXAR** *TOY STORY 4*
THE OFFICIAL MOVIE SPECIAL

**DISNEY** *THE LION KING*
THE OFFICIAL MOVIE SPECIAL

# MARVEL LIBRARY

**X-MEN**
THE DARK PHOENIX SAGA (MAY '20)

### NOVELS
- **ANT-MAN** NATURAL ENEMY
- **AVENGERS** EVERYBODY WANTS TO RULE THE WORLD
- **AVENGERS** INFINITY (NOV '19)
- **BLACK PANTHER** WHO IS THE BLACK PANTHER?
- **CAPTAIN AMERICA** DARK DESIGNS (OCT '19)
- **CAPTAIN MARVEL** LIBERATION RUN (OCT '19)
- **CIVIL WAR**
- **DEADPOOL** PAWS
- **SPIDER-MAN** FOREVER YOUNG
- **SPIDER-MAN** HOSTILE TAKEOVER
- **SPIDER-MAN** KRAVEN'S LAST HUNT
- **THANOS** DEATH SENTENCE
- **VENOM** LETHAL PROTECTOR
- **X-MEN** DAYS OF FUTURE PAST

**MARVEL STUDIOS:**
THE FIRST TEN YEARS

### MOVIE SPECIALS
- MARVEL STUDIOS' *ANT MAN & THE WASP*
- MARVEL STUDIOS' *AVENGERS: ENDGAME*
- MARVEL STUDIOS' *AVENGERS: INFINITY WAR*
- MARVEL STUDIOS' *BLACK PANTHER* (COMPANION)
- MARVEL STUDIOS' *BLACK PANTHER* (SPECIAL)
- MARVEL STUDIOS' *CAPTAIN MARVEL*
- MARVEL STUDIOS' *SPIDER-MAN: FAR FROM HOME*
- MARVEL STUDIOS' THE COMPLETE *AVENGERS*
- MARVEL STUDIOS: THE FIRST TEN YEARS
- MARVEL STUDIOS' *THOR: RAGNAROK*
- *SPIDER-MAN: INTO THE SPIDERVERSE*

### ARTBOOKS
- MARVEL'S *SPIDER-MAN* THE ART OF THE GAME
- MARVEL: *CONQUEST OF CHAMPIONS* THE ART OF THE BATTLEREALM
- *SPIDER-MAN: INTO THE SPIDERVERSE*
- THE ART OF IRON MAN 10TH ANNIVERSARY EDITION

# STAR WARS LIBRARY

- *ROGUE ONE: A STAR WARS STORY* THE OFFICIAL COLLECTOR'S EDITION
- *ROGUE ONE: A STAR WARS STORY* THE OFFICIAL MISSION DEBRIEF
- *STAR WARS: THE LAST JEDI* THE OFFICIAL COLLECTOR'S EDITION
- *STAR WARS: THE LAST JEDI* THE OFFICIAL MOVIE COMPANION
- *STAR WARS: THE LAST JEDI* THE ULTIMATE GUIDE

- *SOLO: A STAR WARS STORY* THE OFFICIAL COLLECTOR'S EDITION
- *SOLO: A STAR WARS STORY* THE ULTIMATE GUIDE
- THE BEST OF *STAR WARS INSIDER* VOLUME 1
- THE BEST OF *STAR WARS INSIDER* VOLUME 2
- THE BEST OF *STAR WARS INSIDER* VOLUME 3
- THE BEST OF *STAR WARS INSIDER* VOLUME 4
- *STAR WARS:* LORDS OF THE SITH

- *STAR WARS:* HEROES OF THE FORCE
- *STAR WARS:* ICONS OF THE GALAXY
- *STAR WARS:* THE SAGA BEGINS
- *STAR WARS* THE ORIGINAL TRILOGY
- *STAR WARS* ROGUES, SCOUNDRELS AND BOUNTY HUNTERS
- *STAR WARS* CREATURES, ALIENS, AND DROIDS
- *STAR WARS: THE RISE OF SKYWALKER* THE OFFICIAL COLLECTOR'S EDITION

**STAR WARS**
THE SAGA BEGINS

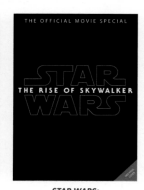

**STAR WARS:**
**THE RISE OF SKYWALKER**
(DECEMBER 2019)

# AVAILABLE AT ALL GOOD BOOKSTORES AND ONLINE

**TITAN**-COMICS.COM | **TITAN**BOOKS.COM